MW00936070

Table of Contents

Dedicated to my lovely wife, Gladys,
my beautiful son, Scott,
and my partners in Jesus Christ at LifePoint,
all of whom have shown me so much
love, support, inspiration, and encouragement
to write and be in ministry today.

Bring Your Brain.

— Me

Prologue

W hy does the world need another book about Christian "answers?" It seems like everywhere you turn, someone is claiming to have all the answers for any and all of life's problems. But I have to say, even with all of the resources out there today, I personally have struggled to find answers that make sense of my deepest questions about life and God. Because of this, for decades now, I have searched and looked and studied, all with the aim of answering *my own questions,* much less those of other people. And like so many people I have known over the years, I began this journey with absolutely no clue where to begin, what to do, or even which questions to ask. While I had at least some exposure to the church and basic Christian doctrine growing up, by my high school years, church (and God) were simply an irrelevant part of everyday life. In the meantime, I did whatever it was I was "supposed to do," which for me, was to pursue an education and a career. Personally, this meant, as was my family tradition, I would do whatever it took in my quest to become a success, including countless hours of study and efforts to open as many doors as possible.

Pursuing a career without God, though, would soon prove to be a frustrating, if not futile, exercise. Like everyone who goes about life without addressing ultimate questions, I found myself in that all too familiar abyss of self-doubt, meaninglessness, and depression. While it was true that I had visions of becoming someone great, underneath my work was the hollow feeling of emptiness. Was this truly all there was, or would be to my life? Was this it? And the irony of ironies was all my efforts to become successful, find meaning, and discover "answers" was actually driving me to frustration. It was making things worse, not helping. Put another way, the irony was that the very pursuit of success, obtaining what I really wanted, and becoming "proficient in life" was in fact driving me to ultimate questions that *my own life pursuits* could not answer. And it was depressing.

So I began to look elsewhere. And I looked. And I read. And I asked. And I studied. And ultimately, I came to believe the answers I was seeking would never be found in "success, career or work," rather they would only be found in God. So I accepted Him. And it was good. But in truth, it was not good enough. I went to church. I looked into Baptist, Catholic, Methodist, and television churches too. I pretty much ran the gamut. Yet still, my questions were not answered. I have always been perpetually plagued by the same question my 5 year old son continually asks me, "Daddy, How come?" That was me, and I guess, even to this day, that is still me. My assumption is that, deep down, all of us want to know "Daddy, How Come?" It's just that we often don't have a clue where to start.

Which leads me to this book. Why another book providing "answers?" My experience is that there simply are not many resources that provide accessible, yet critical answers to our toughest questions. Understand, this book is only intended to be a primer. It is intended to spur you to personal reflection, and hopefully, more in-depth study in the future. For now though, my goal is not to get complicated. You will not find many references, scholarly citations, or links for further study. Instead, it is my goal to make these answers as easy as possible, as logical as possible, yet as profound as possible. Jesus was a master at this--offering truths even a child can understand, yet, when you dig under the surface of those truths, they are so complex even PhD dissertations are surface waves compared to the deep currents that ride underneath.

In finding answers, I owe more than I could ever recognize to Adam Hamilton (Church of the Resurrection in Leawood, KS). Personally, I believe he is one of the best, if not the most profound Christian apologist in the world today, both in the pulpit and in print. Other brilliant thinkers who have influenced my own study are CS Lewis (especially *Mere Christianity*), Lee Strobel (all his *Case For* studies), and Josh McDowell.

To them, I am eternally grateful. My prayer for you is that this study helps you, as much as they have helped me.

Introduction

I will never forget the first time I heard Adam Hamilton's quote, "Don't check your brain at the door when you come into this church." What a contrast to so many Christians who had told me, "sure it contradicts everything you have ever learned, but you just need to have faith!" Yet, when their "faith" brushed against the "truths" of millions, if not billions, of thinking people in this world, it was shallow at best. Are we to really "just have faith" when the truths presented by scientists, anthropologists, or whatever just outright contradict what certain Christians are saying?

You probably know at least a few of the areas of seeming contradiction: dinosaurs, evolution, unanswered prayer, where did God come from? and others. Atheists, agnostics, and antagonists have had a field day with Christians who could not logically answer these and other similar questions. Even worse, because their questions, on the surface, appear so grounded and intelligent, Christians are often categorized as ignorant and weak-minded, if not outright stupid. For many, the inability to answer these questions for themselves has led them away from God or to reject God altogether.

Enter Adam Hamilton, CS Lewis, Lee Strobel, Josh McDowell, and the entire field of Christian apologetics. Make no mistake, these are not weak-minded, stupid people. Neither are they emotionally unstable or schizophrenic. No, they are brilliant, top of their class, calculating, logical, fact-based geniuses. They could be CEOs or professors of any company or university, and they can run with the most distinguished of intellectuals from anywhere on the planet. These apologists could make their case to any seeker or even antagonist, be it Richard Dawkins or Carl Sagan, and come out not only squeaky clean, but, even more, right. If only their answers were promoted, taught and made more accessible to the masses in our educational institutions, but they aren't. And that's just the reality of the society and culture we live in.

True, the basic Christian message is everywhere, and faith in God is so accessible even a child can grasp it. But let's be clear, it is also profoundly riddled with ever-deepening layers of truth that only God Himself fully comprehends. These truths are often not intuitive, and without proper exposure and education, many people will live a lifetime without adequate answers to their deeper questions about God and how God works in our world. Which gets to the gist of it: the nuances of God are not so easily explained, neither are the ways in which He interacts in our world easily understood. Which by the way is exactly why logic, free will, and using our God-given brains are so important. Seriously, why would God give us those things, if He didn't expect us to use them? Why would God give us brains and the ability to process rationally, if he didn't expect us to think logically?

No, God gave you a brain, and my hunch is, God expects you to use it in dealing with life's difficult questions. Where certain antagonists would have you to believe your brain is incompatible with God, the truth is God gave you that brain precisely to lead you to Himself. Science, logic, natural law, free will, genetics, Hubble telescopes, whatever-- these discoveries of human enlightenment should never be barriers to our faith, rather they should enhance, deepen and ground our faith. Being logical should never move you away from God. Rather, it should move you to God. After all, who gave you the ability to think logically in the first place? Some teacher in high school or a professor in college? Or, did God give you that ability?

So that's where we begin. Ask questions. Don't be afraid to look at God and question things. Ask "Why?" Ponder "How Come?" Have faith, yes, but also seek understanding in every area of life that is questionable to you. Questions are good, and, in fact, it is only when you work through those questions with logic, reason and faith that you find your faith becoming truly mature, enduring, deep, profound, vibrant and alive. Make no mistake: your ability to answer your own questions about God and human existence will be the lynchpin upon which your faith stands or collapses. God has given you, and all of us, countless resources (especially our brains) to find answers if we truly desire them. It is God and reason. It is God and logic. It is the God who created logic who will lead us to the ultimate answers we so hunger for and crave when questions of faith and life become relevant for where we live, work, and play.

Don't be afraid to ask, but also, be open to answers that, perhaps, may cause you to stretch a bit. God is God, we are not. The more humbly we both seek out and avail ourselves to His Divine wisdom (instead of trying to justify our own), the more we will find His presence and His Truth become a transforming fire that warms our hearts, brings light to our darkest anxieties and peace and calm to our souls.

CHAPTER 1

What about Hypocrites and the Institutional Church?

Mark 10:27
"It is impossible for human beings. But with God, all things are possible."

L et's begin by just naming the elephant in the room. A large majority of people today are turned off to even *discussing* God because they have been offended by hypocrites in the institutional church. Some are offended by the contradictions between the church and logic (science). Some are offended by the institutional church and money. Others see the abuses of a few churches and walk away from them all. More often than not though, the offense comes through Christians who simply are annoying, intrusive, and so blatantly hypocritical. Far too many people have never even dealt with the important God questions, because they cannot get past the people who claim to be followers of God. Why? It's because, more often than not, it is precisely the hypocritical Christians who have the loudest voices in claiming to have "answers." Why would I listen to *them,* when so clearly they are no better than me? So, let's look at that for a moment before we go any further.

Answer: *All followers of Christ are hypocrites, and that is precisely why we need the church to teach, equip, strengthen, and encourage us to become less hypocritical over time.*

I will never forget my first dose of hypocrisy in the church. It was my freshman year of high school, and for the first time in my life, I was finally beginning to understand just a touch of what faith in Jesus Christ meant. Make no mistake, I was a kid, and I was WAY confused about God and everything else in life. I had big ears, braces, stumbled over my own two feet, and tried desperately to fit in with the cool people. At the same time I also was starting to understand God's love, and it meant a lot to me. I had joined a local church youth group, and was active in that church. I did what they said I should do, including walking the aisle, professing my faith, and being baptized (again). I started reading my Bible. I was singing in the youth choir and going on choir tour. And to be honest, that church was one of the best parts of my life at the time. But something then happened to change all that.

I guess what sticks out most in my mind is how disappointed I was when I found out some of the other kids in the youth group were doing things, and acting in certain ways, that were simply wrong. I don't want to get into specifics in this book, but you can use your imagination as to what young teenagers do that is wrong that they *know* they should not be doing. And I definitely remember being incredibly disappointed when I realized that the kids of my church youth group were actually doing those things on a regular basis. Now, it should be said that I was doing many of the very same things they were. It's just that, in my mind at least, this was *their* church, they had been there long before me and they had the Jesus language to back it up. But here they were, doing the same sinful things I was doing; and then they were going to church on Sunday and acting as if their behavior on Friday and Saturday night didn't matter. At that point, I simply had a disconnect and quit going to church altogether. Little did I know that I was about to experience one of the most difficult events in my life, and the worst part is that I would go through those times without a church or youth group that I could turn to when I needed them most.

It was about a year later that I was enjoying the day in my dad's ski boat on Fish River in south Alabama. Fish River is a great place to water ski. It has tall trees on either side to add protection from the wind. There is always a calm patch of glassy water where you can do tricks without fear of a wave messing up your approach or landing. My brother and I used to ski there all the time. When he graduated, I would take my friends and we would just have a blast. Those are great memories. Except for this one day.

You see, on this particular day, as a few of my friends and I were wrapping up a great afternoon of water skiing, I was driving on the right side of the river as we entered one of those narrow passes. I have always been an extremely careful driver and even to this day have never been in a car accident. The thing is though, unbeknownst to me, there was a boat full of underage kids who had been drinking too much alcohol coming full throttle in my direction on the wrong side (my side) of the river. The boat wasn't just full, but was overloaded, limiting its ability to turn quickly. Laughing and enjoying the wind in my hair, I rounded the corner only to be faced head on with that oncoming boat. For this next part, you need to put yourself behind the steering wheel of a boat at 40 miles per hour rounding the bend of a narrow river. You are surprised, if not stunned, to see an oncoming boat immediately in your path. You turn right, but facing you, they turn left (directly in your path). You turn left, but facing you, they turn right (again, directly in your path). Now you get the picture. For me, in 2 more seconds, if nothing changed, I was going to crash head on at full speed into the oncoming boat. So, from full throttle at 40 miles an hour, I slammed our boat into reverse, cracking the fiberglass transom of our boat. As my boat lurched to a stop, they brushed under my bow, veering the worst way possible, crashing full speed into the pier that was jutting out from the bank immediately beside me.

I will not share the details with you. To be honest, 30 years later, it is hard to revisit. Some pains never heal. We learn to live with them, but healing is another story. I will give this one last piece, because it is relevant: As I pulled the middle school boy out from under the water to unsuccessfully do CPR on him, I have never in my life felt such horror or such loneliness. Where was God in that? Why? To make matters worse, I had no church that really meant something to me to turn to, and I had no answers for the horrific questions about God, no answers about why bad things happen, and why God doesn't answer prayers when you pray someone won't die. For the next five years, it is no understatement to say that I was adrift in a sea of confusion and inner turmoil.

Looking back, I am pretty sure that tragedy had a more profound impact on my life than I probably have ever given credence to. It is interesting to reflect and see that I ran from God for the next 4-5 years or so. Also, it is interesting in reflection today, to ponder the real reasons I think I lived my life the way I did after that difficult season. At that moment, though, can you guess what my excuse was, as to why I could so easily walk away from God and the church? The boating accident? Nope. Too busy? No. To be honest, my primary excuse was, "I am not going back there, because they are all hypocrites." Today, I can only ask God to forgive me for laying my own burdens at the feet of other people's weaknesses. My prayer is that you don't have to go through Hell to learn this all important truth. Which is what?

The simple fact is that followers of Christ *are* hypocrites, but that should never distract us from loving God or enjoying and participating in His church. And, Christians should own the hypocritical part. All of us. Well, all of us who hold Christ as the standard and who attempt to follow His teachings. Why? It's because Jesus raises the bar of ethics, morality, integrity and character so impossibly high that no one could ever live up to it. And here's the thing, if ever you are tempted to walk away from Jesus or the church (we'll get to that in a moment) because of hypocrites in the church, well... don't. Just don't. Why? It's because the church is *necessarily filled* with people who have problems, which means you will fit right in! And me too. After all, Jesus came to heal the sick, not the healthy.

What makes us sick? Many things really, but the main thing is our propensity to just be less than perfect, to say the right thing at the wrong time, or just to outright say the wrong thing. And this is precisely what it means to be human. You might go so far as to say that we sin *because* we're human. The call of Christ though is to try and do better. And as followers of Christ, we *want* to do better, and to strengthen each other as we keep trying. But then we fail again because we're human. But that doesn't change the deep desire to *try* and do better, to *try* and live up to the standards Christ set. Yes, we're hypocrites because we fail to act the way we want to, but we can't stop trying.

So rather than fixing your eyes on the sick people who follow Christ, instead, as the scriptures say, fix your eyes, thoughts, heart and mind on Jesus Himself. Judge Jesus off what Jesus himself says and does, not His followers. And *join* His followers in their journey to do better with their lives. Take your eyes off the hypocrites and put them back where they need to be, on Christ, on God. Listen, don't judge Jesus based off what other Christians say or do. That would be like someone judging you based off what other people said about you, even though they want nothing to do with you. Is that fair? And even more, given the fact that Christians are inherently hypocritical, give them a break. Again, rather than judge them, join them. And why that matters, is because, assuming everyone is operating with at least some semblance of maturity and healthy boundaries, you need them, and they need you too.

You need them in good times. Because it really is fun to hang out with Christian friends who share similar values and are at least attempting to live to a higher standard. You need them to hold you accountable when you miss the mark. You need them to teach you the deeper truths about God you would never figure out on your own. You need them to pray for you and with you. You need them to help teach your children about God. And on and on.

Which brings me to the institutional church. It seems like everyone today is bashing the institutional church. The cry is something like, "well, I believe in God, but not the institutional church." Hmmm. Really? I want to ask, "Tell me, what is it about the institutional church that you don't believe in?" That they at least attempt to show up at the hospital when you are sick or try to be at the funeral of your family member to support you in your time of grief? Is that what you don't believe in? Or, that the church has mission programs that feed the homeless, or feed local school children with snack sacks, or that sends money to help missionaries in Africa who are teaching their people how to feed themselves, read, and write? Is that what you don't believe in? Or that, other than Christian private schools, the church is the only institution left in the entire world that teaches people about Jesus Christ and His message of God's love and grace and hope for all people? Is that what you don't believe in? The government does not teach us or our kids about God. The public schools aren't allowed to. Most universities won't, or if they do, they have to water down the message so much it's nearly irrelevant. The judicial system? Yeah right. And the family unit? Are you teaching your children about God, Jesus Christ, and the fundamental truths of God for our everyday lives? I wish it were so, but reality is that the average family unit doesn't even pray before meals anymore or even sit down as a family to eat. If not the institutional church, who is going to teach us, lead us, call us, and challenge us to love God in a world that no longer cares?

Or from the backside: when you have a horrible tragedy on Fish River, and for the next 5 years of your life you find yourself wandering and questioning and hurting and doubting, but then... Christians (those hypocritical, messed up, dysfunctional, confused Christians) step up beside you and say, "Hey, God loves you. Let me help you with that." And even with all the mess and problems and misguided expectations the whole small group of Christians brings to the table, it helps. It really does. And through that, through those hypocritical, messed up, dysfunctional Christians, you actually see and meet and commune with God. And then, God works a miracle and your soul is healed. And you finally begin to love yourself and see yourself as God sees you... His beloved son, or daughter. And so many other joys happen that I don't have time or space to name. I ask: How could you not believe in that?

Listen, I know the institutional church isn't perfect. Anyone on the inside can tell you that. Are we trying to fix it? Sure. Can it be fixed? Unlikely. Why? Human Condition. Same old problem we've always had. And more to our point, the church can't be ultimately fixed because it is filled with hypocrites. It's just as Jesus said, "I didn't come for the healthy. No, the healthy don't need a doctor. Truth is, I came to heal the sick." And He did heal them, but that doesn't mean all their problems and temptations went away. From the prostitute, to the tax collector, to the blind, to the lame, to the woman suffering from a lifelong hemorrhage to the

Centurion's son, to me. And Jesus can heal you too. Jesus healed them all. But again, the very reason Jesus said "Go your way and sin no more" was precisely because He knew they would be tempted to do the exact opposite as soon as they left His presence. So in point of fact, what Jesus was really saying was, "Now that you have been healed, go your way, and this time... do better... really, really try your hardest, to do better." And I believe they did, just as I do, just as anyone who loves Jesus does too. Put another way, they went their way, and for the first time, they stopped making excuses. And that's what the institutional church and the hypocrites within that church are doing. We are trying to stop making excuses, and we are trying our best to do better, even though we may make the same old mistakes time and time again. And when it all comes out of the wash, my hunch is, that is all God expects of any of us.

Questions for Reflection (and discussion):

1. Have you ever been offended by hypocritical Christians? What was your ultimate response?

2. Have you ever judged God based off what other people said about Him, rather than what you learned or experienced about Him for yourself? When? What did that look like?

3. Has a person of high esteem in the church, or the church itself, ever disappointed you? Did that transfer into your faith in God? If so, how?

4. What would the world look like if the church, and all the ancillary ministries of the church, did not exist? How would that affect what we and our children know about God?

5. What is the value of the institutional church when it is at its best? Can you think of a better option?

6. What is the value of hypocritical, but gracious Christians when they are at their best?

NOTES

CHAPTER 2

Is God Real?

Romans 1:20

*"For since the beginning of time, the creation itself,
the heavens the earth and all that are in it,
have proclaimed the reality of God."*

Have you ever wondered about the reality of God? God, are you there? God, are you anywhere? God, where are you? God, if there is a God, show me... prove yourself to me... because in my life right now, I just don't see it.

Ever feel like that? I know I have. It is especially in times like these (when you question things) that your ability to logically prove the existence of God to yourself can make all the difference in the world. So where to begin?

A. *It had to come from something, somewhere, or Someone.*

To begin understanding God, you must also begin understanding "it." Where did "it" come from? And, the answer, always, lies in the beginning. We go to the starting point of existence and of science, and in fact, the starting point is where science breaks down. That being the Big Bang.

The Big Bang is the prevailing theory of how the Universe began. The short version is at the beginning of time, the Universe was in an extremely hot and dense state and then began expanding rapidly. Scientists can even compute the age of the universe based on how rapidly it is expanding. The Big Bang. Well actually, let's begin from the point of time immediately before the Big Bang. The question I have for you is, where did the matter come from that exploded in the Big Bang? People mock the question. People divert from the question. Some have attempted to avoid the question. But the question remains, "Tell me, where did that initial matter that exploded in the Big Bang come from?"

And you know the saying, "The most obvious answer is usually the correct answer." So you tell me, what's the most obvious answer? For any logical, thinking person, we all know the truth that particles/things/matter simply cannot appear out of thin air. "Things" don't appear out of "Nothing." Someone, something, some anything had to create the matter at the Big Bang. And I don't care how you slice it or how many diversionary tactics you use, there is no argument in all of existence that can make sense of matter magically appearing out of thin air. Things don't appear out of thin air. It had to come from someone, somewhere, somehow. What makes more sense? To say God created the particles, or to say they magically appeared out of thin air? Simple logic here is obvious: God created it, and it did not magically appear out of thin air. I don't believe in magic, and neither should you.

And by the way, for those who ask, "well fine, then where did God come from?" Not too difficult either, as God is infinite. It is an illogical question to ask, "where did the infinite come from?" By nature, the infinite has no beginning and no end. Now, if you want to say that all matter of the universe is infinite, then, fair enough. But that is another question entirely that ought to be tackled by scientists. And for now, the scientific community is clearly saying the universe is not infinite, rather it had a clear, one-time beginning at the Big Bang. So until the majority of scientists tell us otherwise, we will dialogue within the parameters of truth they themselves set for us.

B. *Who turned the key?*

I love cars. I have always loved cars. I will never forget, as a child in the 70s, riding in the backseat of my dad's Pontiac Trans Am. It was the same car Burt Reynolds drove in *Smoky and the Bandit*. And I know, I am dating myself. But did I mention I love cars?

My good friend Steve is a master mechanic. Steve owns a Muscle-car shop, and honestly, if I weren't a pastor, I might ask Steve for a job. He puts superchargers on cars, he upgrades manifolds and intakes, he dyno tests them ... Steve is cool. But here's the thing: Steve can assemble all the cars he wants. He can make a 400+ horsepower Corvette Stingray into a 1100 horsepower monster. But the thing is, if no one ever gets into the car and actually turns the key, it will never run.

How much more complicated is the universe than a Muscle-car? How much more complicated are the stars in the sky, the galaxies of the universe, or even the nuances of the butterfly or life itself compared to any car? And yet, any 5-year-old kid can tell you, a car will not start, unless someone turns the key.

So goes the universe. Someone had to flip the ignition switch. Big Bang... great! But, engines don't crank by themselves. Someone has to turn the key. This is not rocket science, rather this is elementary science. Who flipped the ignition switch to the Big Bang? The most logical answer is God.

C. *Who gave it gas?*

Ever run out of gas? Not a good place to be. I have only run out of gas one time in my life, and it was a freezing cold day with my baby son in the car AND we were in the middle of a major highway. It was not fun. The thing is, on that day, I would have given ANYTHING if my car would have run without gas. In fact, I tried to crank it for about 10 extra minutes just hoping gas would magically appear. Then, with magic gas, my car could run to the nearest gas station. I prayed, I hoped, I begged, I pleaded, I talked to the car, I talked *at* the car (if you know what I mean), but gas never appeared. My car never cranked while the needle was on "E," and my hunch is, it never will.

Am I really supposed to believe that the biggest explosion in the history of the cosmic order happened on "E"? When my own car engine will not "fire" without a little gas, am I somehow supposed to believe that the Big Bang did? Or, that the single greatest fiery explosion of epic proportions happened without someone filling the fuel tank prior to that explosion?

The thing is, explosions require energy. We all know this. Whether it be the explosion of a cylinder head in an engine bay, the explosion of fireworks, the explosion of a rifle bullet, or the explosion of the Big Bang. The scriptures often refer to God as light, even energy. When Moses encountered God, he shone like light (pure energy). When Jesus was transfigured, He too shone like pure light. Coincidence? Perhaps. But perhaps, as the scriptures say, God *is* light, which also means God is energy. Where did the energy for the Big Bang come from? Where does ALL of the energy for the universe ultimately come from? From magic, from nothing? Unlikely. From God? That is the only answer that makes sense.

D. *Where did the spark come from?*

So, ok. You assemble the car, you fill it up, and you turn the key. Fantastic. Good for you. But, you still need a spark, or it's all for naught.

Have you ever been to a truly fantastic July 4th fireworks display? Down in south Alabama, every year at Fort Rucker, the military puts on an awesome fireworks display. For the entire day before the evening fireworks show, there are vendors, cotton candy, hotdogs and bratwurst, several performance stages with bands, helicopters to walk in, etc. Lots of fun. But the main attraction is the fireworks. And early in the day, people will setup their lawn chairs, put out their blankets, and mark their spot for the best seats possible to watch the fireworks. And at some point, the professionals come out and setup the fireworks. As dusk approaches and the day turns to darkness, the show soon arrives. But what we know is those fireworks will not go "BANG!" without someone putting them out there, providing a spark of flame and lighting the fuse. They just don't, and it is nonsense to think they ever would.

Can't you just hear God the Father talking to Jesus immediately before the greatest fireworks display in the history of the cosmos? Perhaps it went like this. In the beginning, before the beginning in fact, God through Christ created and perfectly assembled the world's largest Roman candle. They carefully transport it to its final resting place before the big show, and they add the final touch of explosives and fuel to make it go boom. They have carefully setup a safe zone. The angels are all in their lawn chairs eating popcorn and brats, having been listening to the heavenly July 4th bands all day and visiting with friends and family. As anticipation builds, darkness falls upon the land signaling that the time is near. The Father, Jesus, and the Spirit are seen moving over the waters. They carefully approach the preset fireworks display in the middle of the arena. You see God giving Jesus the "thumbs up" sign, which in essence flips the switch that readies the engine to the "on" position. LONG PAUSE. Wait for it. Wait for it. Then Jesus yells, "FIRE IN THE HOLE!" and he comes running at breakneck speed back to the safe zone... and then....
"BBBBAAAAANNNNNGGGGGGG!!!!!!!!!!!!!!!!!!!!!!!"
And the universe was started. And all the angels and Jesus

and the Father and everyone went, "Ahhh... Ohhhhh.... Wowwww!"

However you want to describe it. Someone had to provide the spark that would light the fuse. That Someone, was God.

E. *Someone had to design, program, and assemble the whole thing.*

This is the final piece. And don't get hung up on the details of *how* God designed it. For us, what matters most is *that* God designed it. It makes no sense to say everything in the entire created order assembled itself in such a way that it could run itself once it was started. It makes no sense to say, all by itself, from complete chance and random accident, the universe, with all of its complexities, came into being.

Buildings require architects. Casseroles require both a recipe and a chef. Clothes require a designer. But, especially those programs that run continually after startup, they require a programmer. And on and on and on. Listen, programs don't program themselves, and even the ones that come close always had to have an initial programmer. Anything else is not logical. So, if it is true in everyday life, it is probably true pretty much everywhere. Why would the creation of the universe work any differently than the creation of a computer or whatever else in our lives today? Logically, it wouldn't. If that were honestly true, then shouldn't a new IPad assemble itself in your office, with a new Porsche in your garage, and a new theatre room in your attic? If only! But who is going to wait around for that to happen? No one, because it's ludicrous to even halfway believe such a thing. And we are supposed to believe that about *everything?* Truth is, it takes a whole lot more faith to believe the universe designed, programmed, and assembled itself than to simply accept God did it all.

Understand, we, even Christians, can debate *how* God did it all day long. 7 days, 13+ billion years, dinosaurs, no dinosaurs, flood, no flood, no form of evolution at all, or God put the entire evolutionary scheme into place and let it go... whatever, that's not the point. The point *is* that incredibly complicated things don't assemble themselves by themselves. And, they are inherently governed by an internal design and structure. And, design and structure do not appear from a vacuum. Instead, structure and design require thought and intelligence, which when considering the cosmos could only come from God. Seriously, who or what else could it be? Aliens? Give me a break. Which only leaves two options: either God did it, or "nothing" did it. To say the most infinitely complicated design which spans the far reaches of the cosmos all happened by "nothing" almost borderlines absurdity. The odds of it all happening by pure chance and accident are so astronomically impossible that you might as well believe that cows also jump over the moon. Not even the Chick-Fil-A cows can do that. Once again, this leaves God as the only viable option. For most thinking people, God is the correct and most logical answer regarding the design and intelligence behind the structure and systems of the created order.

Conclusion: *Which leaves us where?*

God just make sense. Before we even get to other questions, the initial question of God's existence must be addressed. Does God exist? Is God real? Does God's existence make sense for a thinking person? And the answer?

Of Course! Or as my friend likes to say, "Duh!" Of course God exists, and of course it makes more logical sense to believe that God is real than any other option available to us, thinking people. There is not an argument in the entire world that makes more sense than this claim to the reality of God. For the other questions we have, we will get to that. For now, I hope you will pause and reflect on the above arguments and your own belief in God.

Do you believe that God is real? And if so, "Daddy, how come?"

Questions for Reflection (and discussion):

1. Do you have any experiences which point to the existence of God?

2. What did Paul mean in Romans when he wrote that the creation proclaims the reality of God?

3. Who do you know that firmly believes God exists? What are their reasons?

4. How do the discoveries of science actually help us believe in God?

5. Setting the arguments about "how" God created aside for a moment, does it make sense to say God created it all in the first place? If so, what logical reasons make sense of this for you?

NOTES

CHAPTER 3

Why am I here?

Gen 2:18

"It is not good to be alone."

S o it starts with God. But once you prove God exists, then you simply must ask the question: Well, if God exists, and if God created it all, then why did God create me? The questions go something like: Why am I here? What am I supposed to be doing with my life? Why does my life feel so meaningless and insignificant at times? Shouldn't there be more? Shouldn't my life be more than this?

Answer: *Of course your life is more "than that." It is simply a matter of understanding why you were created in the first place.*

Several Christmases ago, my parents had the brilliant idea of buying an 8-foot long toy bulldozer for my son. I didn't know they had done it until I showed up at their house for Christmas week and they explained their excitement over this fabulous new toy from the tractor supply store. My son was 3 at the time and so all I could think of was how much he would enjoy the gift (and not what this implied for *me*). I thanked them profusely and marveled at the size of the 49 foot box that was nestled under their 7 foot Christmas tree.

Well, come time to open presents, and to no one's surprise, my son made a bee-line to the biggest box. And sure enough, he was thrilled once the wrapping paper was torn off and this beautiful, magnificent picture of a fully assembled bulldozer emerged. Which of course, he wanted to ride and play with immediately. The only problem was, after renting the crane it took to reach the top of the box to open it, I soon discovered that the beautiful, magnificent bulldozer on the outside of the box looked NOTHING like the bazillion pieces of plastic, stickers, screws and bolts that were inside the box. And I looked back at my parents, and they just laughed and laughed and laughed.

And I worked. And I slaved. And I sweated. And I studied. And I summoned all of my clear and unquestioned God-given brilliance and ingenuity to assemble that bulldozer. And when I was done, I threw my hands in the air, chanted around the bonfire, and proclaimed myself the pinnacle of the human species. Except. Except for this one little plastic piece. I thought to myself in righteous purity, "Hmmm, I wonder what that beautiful, little, yellow plastic piece is for? But clearly I didn't need it, or I would have put it on the bulldozer already." And I reveled even more in my moment of glory for having assembled an entire bulldozer by myself, with no formal experience or training. And of course, all this without the need for instructions.

And the angels were singing, and the sun was shining in my little cocoon of glory until my son got on the bulldozer and attempted to use it. Specifically, he wanted to use the scoop. You see, the scoop is lifted up and lowered down, by a beautiful, little, pretty, yellow, plastic piece. And without that plastic piece, the entire show..... as CS Lewis says, "conks." And yes, after a few choice words of disparity, and perhaps a few more choice thoughts that bordered on outright unwholesomeness that does not befit my priestly role, I disassembled pretty much the entire bulldozer, put the plastic piece where it belonged, reassembled the entire thing, and cursed righteously the entire time.

So here's the thing: On the outside, so many of our lives can look really pretty and picture perfect. And even more, as we grow up and move through the various stages of life, we can even begin to put the various pieces of our lives together that appear to us to be in the right places. And we can convince ourselves, for a season at least, that our lives are going to work great "looking like that." But here's the challenge: when it comes to scooping dirt, when it comes to the heavy lifting that happens when life gets tough, well... if all the pieces are not in the right place, your life simply conks, it won't work. And no amount of sincerity, trying hard, or hoping in the future will fix it. To truly fix your life, all the correct pieces must be in their proper place. Especially, the most fundamental piece of all--knowing why you are here in the first place.

Thus the question: "How come?" "Why?" Can you answer it? Why are you here, what are you supposed to be doing, what is your purpose in life? Assuming God exists now, why did God create you? And the answer is, as cliché as it may sound, you exist to love.

Several problems exist when using the word "love" to address the question of human existence though. "Love" is so often abused and misunderstood in our culture that I am uncertain even using the term is helpful. You have love between friends, which is different from love between spouses, which is different than love between parents and children, which is different than love between a person and their dog, etc. But one point CS Lewis clearly makes in his book *Mere Christianity* is that, for most of us, few things are more misunderstood than our concept of love. We think love is about sweaty palms and going out to movies. We think love is about a feeling you have with someone else in Hawaii or at your favorite restaurant. We love based on how wonderful the other person makes us feel, and the incredible times you have together. The problem is that love is not really any of those things. No wonder there is something like a 50% divorce rate in our society today. No wonder so many people who are currently married are miserable. And it is depressing.

Love is not just about passion or feelings. Yes, for many it can start out that way, but love that truly endures always transforms into something far deeper and far more powerful. Which is what exactly? Love is nothing more, and nothing less, than what any two healthy, awesome parents would feel for their newborn child the first time they hold him or her in their arms. Perhaps it's a little hard to describe, but it is palpable nonetheless... it is a love called "grace."

Grace. Grace is yet another word that has been so overused and abused it has become cliché. And, far too many people really don't understand what it means. What is it? Grace is the unconditional, undeserved, unmerited love of one person for another. Grace. It is that one "part" of life that is so fundamental, if you miss it, your entire life conks. And just like every other truth about God that speaks to the heart, we learn about it through our everyday life experiences... like when we have kids. Certainly, you don't need to have kids to understand grace or true love, it's just the principle that matters.

Can I describe for you the experience of holding my son in my arms the very first time? Can I put into words on a piece of paper what it meant to me and my wife when, after Scott was born, how, in that moment, we simply wept because the deep sense of love we felt that words could not express? Can I possibly explain to you how that pivotal moment of Scott's birth in our marriage changed us, both as individuals and as a couple? The question, though, is, why? Seriously, why would we love our newborn son at all? I mean, at 1 day old, had he done anything for us? Had he vacuumed the carpet, cleaned the dishes, or made daddy proud by scoring that touchdown? Had he made his straight As, aced the SAT and gone on to graduate from Yale with honors? Had he done anything for me? No. Nothing. And yet, I knew in that moment, I loved him so much I would die for him if it ever came to it. And to this day, I still believe I would do it. I love him so much, sometimes it literally hurts.

If this sounds reminiscent of Jesus on the cross, it should. If it sounds like Jesus saying to us, "Greater love no one has, than to die for your friends. And you are my friends." Well, "it" should. And what "it" is, is in fact the final piece, it is the pivotal bolt on the proverbial tractor scoop. "It" is the bolt that brings our entire lives into order, offering meaning, giving us purpose and significance. It is grace. It is unconditional love, true love. That overused, often misunderstood, yet unbelievably important truth that grounds our faith and our lives, both in the present and in the eternal life to come.

The Bible makes it clear that God is a personal, loving, gracious God. Through stories like the prodigal son, Jesus makes it clear that God considers us His children, even when we stray like lost sheep. And God loves us. God loves you. Unconditionally. Without regard for your grades, your income, the car you drive or the clothes you wear. Without regard for whether you were popular in high school or if you became the star quarterback, or even if you are a drug addict, a prostitute or an alcoholic. Would I be disappointed in my son (or daughter) if he did those things? Of course. But would I love him any less? Never. God's grace is like that, only infinitely more genuine and profound. It is the same love I have for my son, only with far more depth than we can ever truly grasp.

Now why that matters is because it gets to the purpose of our existence in the first place. **'Why are you here?'** Simple, God wanted kids. And why would anyone want kids? Some of you may be thinking, "Honestly Thomas, I have no idea at this moment why I wanted kids." But be serious, and think carefully on this one, because sometimes we miss it. It is the same reason any healthy person would get married. It is NOT because of feelings or passion (we all know that comes and goes). It is not because of the touchdowns or the accolades. No, it is because God wanted to share life and to share meaning with us. This is why healthy parents have kids. This is why healthy marriages and healthy friendships last a lifetime. It is because we know, it is not good to be alone. And we also know, it is good to share life, ALL of life, the highs and lows, good times and horrible times.

It is so very good to go through all of life together. To have someone always by your side. To have someone share every ounce of life with you, when you are healthy and when you have cancer, when you are a jerk and when you have your act together--to share it all. Sharing life and sharing meaning with God, not because of what He will do for us or for what we will do for him, but because of who He is and who you are too. You are his son. You are his daughter. Until we actually hear it in person, "Welcome home, welcome home."

So, why are you here? Again, "how come?" Please, tell me... why? And my answer for you: Love. Get this, and in a very real way, everything else in life will work much, much more smoothly. Get this, and the colorless fabric of your existence will transform into a deeper tapestry of beauty and grace.

Questions for Reflection (and discussion):

1. Why *are* you here? What is your ultimate purpose in this life? In the life to come?

2. Why do most people value family? What is it about family that *you* value?

3. How do your understandings of (healthy) family teach you about your reason for living? How do your understands of family teach you about God?

4. Name the different types of love you have experienced in life. What is the difference between those "loves" and grace?

5. If God looks at you with grace, how might that affect how you look at God?

NOTES

CHAPTER 4

Why Doesn't God Answer My Prayers?

Psalm 22:2
*"O my God, I cry out by day,
but you do not answer"*

O K, so God exists. Got it. And God created me because of grace - because God wanted to love and be loved, because God wanted to share life and life experiences with me. Got it. But seriously, how can I believe in an all-loving, and all-powerful "Creator of the universe" God who loves me like that, when God doesn't answer my prayers when I need Him the most? If God really loves me like that, then why doesn't He truly help me when I ask Him for help? Or if not me, then other people when I pray for them?

Is that ever you? If so, you're not alone. Millions if not billions of people over time have thought the very same thing and had the very same questions. And please understand, having those thoughts is not wrong or "out of line." Even King David had those same thoughts when he wrote Psalm 22. It is not horrible to think such things or have such questions. In fact, per this entire study, I say it again, questions are good. And the depth of your faith will be proportionately affected by your ability to answer these tough questions. So given that, let's talk about unanswered prayer for a moment.

The Point: *God answers prayer. But, God also set the rules, so God's answers to our prayers usually come in unexpected ways that don't "break the rules" God Himself made.*

Football. American pastime. No question, many people in our society have turned an entertaining sport into a diseased obsession. But laying that aside for a moment, some of my fondest memories of "family time" are when me, my brother, mom and dad would load up in the van and traverse 3 hours of south Alabama roads to my granddad's house to gather for the annual Iron Bowl.

No pro football teams or pro baseball teams exist in Alabama. You never hear of the Alabama NHL Hockey team winning the Stanley Cup or the Birmingham Basketball team winning the NBA Championship. Nope. All we have is football, and especially college football. More specifically, Alabama and... whatever that other team is.... oh yeah, Auburn.

Now, the only little problem in this family scenario is that, even though many in the family are Alabama fans, my mom went to Auburn, my Aunt went to Auburn, my other

Aunt loves Auburn, many of my cousins love Auburn, etc. The Iron Bowl is the annual football rivalry between Alabama and Auburn. So when we gather for the Iron Bowl, in truth, there is the potential for my mom and Aunt to be rolling around on the floor fighting with my Uncles or brother or whoever. Fingers in eyeballs, pulling of hair, etc. There is the potential for popcorn to fly and children to start screaming and drinks to get knocked over ... you get the picture. But here is what holds it all in check, and here is what keeps it fun: The Rules.

Rules. In the game of football, what are the rules? Well, something like, "You are allowed to do this, and you are not allowed to do that. You can grab a player's pads, but you cannot grab their facemask. You can get in front of a receiver to bat the ball away, but you cannot interfere with his route, etc." And the thing is, as long as both Alabama and Auburn players stick within the rules, my family truly does remain civil and the game is fun. Additionally, as long as my family sticks within the rules of fair play in *watching* the game, the game is fun too.

There is an interesting dynamic though when one of the players from "the other team" seems to get away with a blatant, game changing foul and it is not called. And it doesn't happen often. But a few times over the last 30 years that I can remember, there was a major "foul" that was not called that probably changed the outcome of the game. And not just for the game, but also for the family dynamic in watching the game. When it does happen, good clean fun and "ribbing" often turns toxic. People start yelling at the refs, outcries of "That was a foul! What moron can't see that was a foul! That's not fair! What was he thinking!, etc." If instant replay doesn't fix the bad call, then no matter who wins the game, both sides look back to the "foul" as the pivotal point where "things would have been different 'if only'....

Why do we have rules both in football, in society, and even in life? Do we realize that without rules, life would be a chaotic mess of unpredictability that would make every single day pretty much impossible to enjoy? Think about it. What if you truly had no idea what to expect the next time you got in your car to drive to the grocery store? What if there were no rules for the road and people could drive on any side of the road, at any speed, with no blinkers, no stop signs, no right of way, no anything... would you like that? Or, when you got to the grocery store, what if there were no parking stripes and no buggy. When you got inside, what if all the items were just dumped in a huge pile with no price tags. If you even found what you wanted, when you got to the checkout line, what if they arbitrarily made up whatever prices they wanted for the food you were buying. No rules, anything goes. Would you like that?

Answer: *Of course not. We like rules. We like order. We like structure, in fact, we crave it. For without rules, there is no predictability. And without predictability, life spirals into chaos, unfairness and frustration.*

God is not a God of chaos. God is not a God of downward spirals of unfairness and frustration. God is fair and just and so God created rules. God's rules are not (as some antagonists think) to "tell us what to do" or to "glory in ruling from on high." God put rules in place so that we could have predictability, structure, and various other things that lead to peace. This includes moral and ethical rules (like "Do Unto Others"). But it also includes the physical laws, or rules, that govern the universe. These are rules that govern cause and effect, the periodic table, gravity, and so many other things that make our world a fairly predictable place to live.

The next question then is, who is responsible for the Laws of Physics? The physicists who discovered them, or the God that created them? Who is responsible for the Laws of Gravity? The scientist who had an apple fall on his head, or the God who created the apple? Now listen closely, because this is where it gets critically important: Why would God break His own rules (of Natural Law) that God Himself created to help us have order, structure, and predictability in life? Put another way, why would God break God's own rules that were given to us as a gift to help us avoid chaotic, frustrating, unfair, unpredictable lives? Sure, certain things in life are not fair. Read *Job* or *Ecclesiastes* if you want a dissertation on the unfairness of life. But can you imagine how incredibly unfair life would become if in fact there was absolutely no predictability to the natural order of things?

Natural Law. Physics. Cause and Effect. A person gets drunk and drives, and chances are, they or someone else gets seriously hurt or worse. But if everyone obeys the rules, no one ever gets killed by a drunk driver. Natural Law. Physics. Cause and Effect. If you smoke too much, you run a high risk of lung cancer. If no one smoked, then no one would ever get lung cancer from smoking. Natural Law. Physics. Cause and Effect. When people make poor choices, other people are usually negatively affected. When people make poor choices, usually *they* are negatively affected. Natural Law. Physics. Cause and Effect. When the heat and cold and moisture and wind patterns rise off the ocean and it collides with certain thermal conditions, hurricanes ensue, and often we humans are in their path.

Sometimes bad things just happen due to the risk inherent to the physical world and the Natural Laws we live in- tornadoes, hurricanes, earthquakes, famine, pestilence. It is ridiculous that our current insurance policies still call these "Acts of God," as if God is spinning hurricanes. What do we know? God isn't choosing to punish people who live in a coastal community. People live in the coastal community to be near the ocean and the associated food, commerce, employment, beaches, and other positive qualities. But those very people know there is risk associated with living near the water, and those people also accept the risks that come with such great rewards. "Acts of God" is simply not true. Any thinking person knows: all these things are simple cause and effect quite explainable by the physicists, scientists, and chemists among us.

We can then take this a step further, by observing that the Natural Laws God Himself created will in turn *usually set the rules* for how God Himself is going to work in our lives. In this, it's not that God cannot break His own rules whenever God so chooses. It is, however, that 99 times out of 100, that's not the way God works. If God decided to literally start using a magic wand to move this mountain from here to there, then so be it. God is God, and we are not Him. But more often than not, to move that mountain, God is going to operate within the rules of physics that God himself put into place. This then would require us to pick up a shovel, and with God's help, to move that pile of dirt from here to over there.

Unanswered Prayer. Do your unanswered prayers usually involve asking God to wave a magic wand, *God* move the mountain, and in so doing, change the rules? When your prayers have gone unanswered in the past, would your prayers have required God to flex his 'supernatural, magic power' to change the rules of the natural order? If so, I just call the question: Is that fair? Is it really fair, in the middle of a football game, to say to the ref, "you need to change the rules for this one play, because I love this team... and I want them to win."

Think about it long enough, and you will see that *expecting* God to change the rules for you just makes no sense. Asking God to answer any particular prayer *within* the rules that God created? Better. Put another way, maybe it is helpful to consider this in terms of free will. Part of the rules of love that God set in place is that we must also have the choice to hate. Love is not love if there is not true free will to choose the opposite. I wonder though, for people who *pray* that God would break the rules so "that person will come back to me," do they really know what they are saying?

Just imagine if, when we prayed, God manipulated people's free will like a puppeteer pulling the puppet strings. What if God *forced* you to marry that idiot in high school that you could not stand simply because they prayed it so? What if God manipulated *your* free will anytime anyone prayed for you to do something? Not good. Maybe a better approach is to assume God *will* answer prayer, just within the rules He created that do not manipulate free will or natural law. Which implies, answers will happen, but more than likely in ways you don't expect. As Garth Brooks so eloquently sang, "Sometimes I thank God for unanswered prayers. Remember when your talkin' to the Man upstairs, that just because He doesn't answer, doesn't mean He don't care."

So pray. And trust God's promises to answer your prayers. But pray with the understanding that God usually works in ways we can't understand. While also, God usually works in ways we *can* understand, that being within the rules God gave us, because that is one way God keeps the playing field fair. And seriously, if God did that for you, then what about the other team? What about the other 6+ billion people on the planet? If God changed the rules God put in place every time every person on this 6+ billion person planet made a request to change free will or Natural Law, what kind of chaos would that be like? It would be a living Hell down here. If we are honest with ourselves, none of us would truly want that.

What God *does* when we pray:

1. Prayer provides balance and perspective to our lives;
2. Prayer allows God's Spirit to guide us into the best possible outcome within the rules of free will and the Natural Order;
3. Prayer sets the vision (Thy Kingdom, on earth as it is in heaven), vision sets the destination, and destination gives direction for where we are going and what we need to be doing to get there;
4. Prayer reminds us who we are, as God's children, which in turn transforms life from a cosmic orphanage to being part of a greater, kingdom family with God as our Father;
5. Prayer calms the storms of our lives, from the daily rain clouds to the life-altering tsunamis;

6. When we pray, God's Spirit literally takes our burdens and in their place ushers in peace for our souls, no matter the storms that rage around us;

7. Prayer helps us remember, and remembering creates in us humility and gratefulness, and humility and gratefulness are foundation stones for true joy and happiness in life;

8. Prayer connects us to the Vine, which in turn fills us with the Spirit, who allows us to bear God's fruit of peace, joy, hope, love, gentleness, kindness, faithfulness, and more;

9. And yes, God does physically answer our prayers when we pray too. Often not in our timing, and often not in ways we expect, but He most certainly answers them nonetheless as only God can do.

Which matters regarding unanswered prayer... exactly how? It is my personal belief that, for the vast majority of people, when they pray, they are not thinking in terms of the nine points above. Instead, they are simply asking God to break the rules. When most people pray, they are saying, "God, I know real life doesn't work this way, I know Natural Law and the physical rules that govern the Universe don't work this way, so I am asking you to please break those rules for me. I know free will doesn't work this way, but God, please do this one thing for me." Why? Because I have a need. Why? Because, in this particular situation, I am not satisfied to live within the normal rules, that You created, that govern every other aspect of my life (that, by the way, I appreciate). Yes, I know I need the rules in all the other areas because they provide me predictability, but in this case, I don't appreciate them, because they are making some aspect of my life miserable.

Please don't hear me wrong on this point. God is God and God is sovereign. As such, God can break whatever rules that God created whenever He wishes. Certainly, God can and does work in our physical world for good. And, always, always, God answers prayer. He is working among us, in us, around us, and He is faithful to keep His promises as only He can. Our challenge, though, is to not interpret God's promises in whatever ways we believe suit our best interests. In truth, we really don't even know (big picture) what our best interests are. As Jesus says, God will not give you a stone when you ask for a piece of bread, just as God will not give your kid a snake when they ask for a donut. The key? Let God be God. Trust that the rules He put in place are in the best interests of all of us. And, as only God can do, He will work both within and around those rules as He sees fit to accomplish what is in the best interests of everyone when it is all said and done.

So can you answer the question: Why doesn't God answer my prayers when I pray? Daddy, why? Daddy, how come?

Questions for Reflection (and discussion):

1. Have you had unanswered prayer in your own life? Did it affect your faith in God? How?

2. In looking at unanswered prayer, how many of those prayers were related to God changing Natural Law or free will?

3. Evaluate your own prayer life. Today, how often are your prayers focused on God changing Natural Law or free will?

4. For all 6+ billion people on the planet, if God answered all of our prayers to change Natural Law and free will in our favor *every time every person* prayed, what would that look like?

5. Consider the 9 points on what God *does* when we pray. Which of those points do you relate to the most? Which points could you learn from?

NOTES

CHAPTER 5

Is Heaven Real? (And if so, why should I care?)

John 14:1-2
"Trust God, and Trust Me.
If it weren't real,
I would have told you so."

OK, so God exists. Check. And God created me to share life with Him. Check. And, God answers all prayer, just in His way. Check. But I still have questions. I mean, what about Heaven? Is heaven for real? And, also, what about Hell? Seriously, how can God be all loving and send people to Hell? And how can God consider all of us "His children" and love us unconditionally (grace), if some of those children don't have the same opportunity to get into heaven as others? It just doesn't seem right to me.

Answer: *If God is real, then heaven is real.*

Coming home. It really can be a great thing. Granted, most of our homes are filled with dysfunction at varying levels, and most of us have "issues" that cloud the greatness that a "perfect homecoming" might be. But even with all of that, having a place to call home, having a place where you know you are welcome, having a place where you fit, having a house, a kitchen, a fridge, a closet, a room that is yours, it truly is one of the greatest gifts we have. And more, to fill that place with other people who truly love you... even better.

To understand Heaven and Hell, and to answer questions about those places, you also have to understand home. What makes a home home? What makes a certain space your home, verses any other space? What makes you more comfortable (ideally) at home than any other place in the world? Why do I look forward to both being at home and going home for Christmas? What's so special about home anyway?

And I think the saying is true, that home is where the heart is. Ideally, home is that place in our world where you can let your guard down and know that the people in the space accept you for who you are. Home is that place where, you cannot put on pretenses, you can't act like you are "all that," because the other people there know you aren't. And yet, they love you anyway and they accept you anyway. And it doesn't matter how long you have been gone, when you arrive home, there is always a hug and a smile and an open door that says, "you belong here." You never have to ask permission to go home. You never have to ask permission to go the fridge or to turn on the TV. Home is home, and we all long for a place to truly call home.

But that longing also points out part of the tragedy of "home" too. Because so often, given that we do know the ins and outs of everyone's problems, home can quickly feel more like an ideal than reality. For far too many people, home is not where the heart is, rather home is where the dysfunction and the abuse and the bad memories are. Home is the place where flaws are exposed and old sins remain unforgiven and on and on and on... and it hurts. We long for the ideal. We have what is real. For many, their experience of home lies somewhere in-between.

Concerning matters of heart and home, it is important to remember that life often forces us to note the difference between reality and the ideal. I say "note," but much stronger language could be used. Life doesn't just force us to "note" inconsistencies between reality and the ideal, often life so sucks the wind from your sails that we question whether or not the ideal even exists. Fair enough. But here's the thing: What if one of God's tools for helping us understand ideal "reality" is in fact our experiences of everything that is less than ideal in our lives today? Ideal reality. That's a thought for you, that the ideal *is* the reality, while reality is in fact a shadow.

Let me word it this way. As CS Lewis teaches in his Chronicles of Narnia book series (especially *The Last Battle*), we are given a picture of the "most true reality" when the Bible teaches us about our ultimate reality in heaven. Heaven is the final destination. Heaven is the only reality that is in fact constant, verses our current reality that is a fading piece of grass in the field. As James 4:14 says, life down here is a mist, a vapor in the wind. It is a shadow, a passing wisp or breath. Heaven, on the other hand, is the true world without end, and our world down here is but a shadow, a foretaste, of that one. Do we get glimpses of what is to come of that one in this one? Sure. But as Lewis states, when we get there, that world will be so incredibly real, that this life will seem as little more than a passing dream compared to the dense and thick beauty of that one. The Apostle Paul adds that not one human being has ever seen, heard, or even imagined how amazing heaven will be. It simply is too far beyond our present sufferings and imperfections to comprehend.

So, how does this relate to home? And why should I care? And for *this* answer, we simply need to assemble a few building blocks that were established in our previously mentioned questions. We start with the existence and nature of God. God does exist, and He is, by nature, the embodiment of love and grace. We also know, by being the embodiment of love, God desires to share meaning and life with others, including us, which is why God "had" or created us human beings in the first place. In a very real but simplistic way, God wanted children, which then clearly implies that God wanted a family, an extended family, a BIG family to share life and meaning with.

Which then brings us to the ultimate question on this one: If God wanted a family to share life with, and if one of the fundamental purposes of our existence is to share that existence with God, then where are we ultimately going to share that existence with God? In our homes, or in His? Think about it. Assuming you buy into the reality of God, then clearly God has to exist somewhere. The question is, where? And the scriptures tell us, as Jesus also taught us to pray, "Our Father, who art... in... *heaven*." Christian doctrine understands heaven to be God's home, or interchangeably, the Kingdom of Heaven is the Kingdom of God, which is exactly where God the Father resides.

Let's go over that in a little more detail. Jesus said, when you pray, pray "Our Father...." *Our*, meaning a greater community of human beings who are children of God and whom God is Father (a better translation of that word, *Abba*, is probably dad, daddy, pop, poppa, etc.). And then, "Who art in *heaven.*" Jesus is saying, God, Our Father, resides in heaven. Why did He tell us to pray that way? To teach and continually remind us of both the vision and the eternal destination to which all of "us" (the "*our*" part) are ultimately headed. This is where our Father resides, which is where His, thus our, residence is too. Which brings us to the place of both home and family.

Heaven is the place where God's family lives. In John 14, Jesus says that we are not to worry and we are not to be afraid. Why? Because he promised to go and prepare a place for "you." For in the Father's house (home), there are many rooms. Rooms for whom? God's family. And later, Jesus promises to take us to be there, so that we can all be together, where we were created to live in the first place. Which finally gets us to the meat in answering our initial questions about Heaven and Hell.

Is heaven real? Answer: Heaven is as real as God is real. And if you can prove God exists, then you have corollary proof that heaven exists too. Why? If you believe God is real, and if you also believe God, as Father, exists in a place not of this world, then whatever that place is, must be real too. And thus, heaven is as real as God is real, because wherever God the Father lives, is exactly what heaven, or the Kingdom of God, is. Thus, the reality of God necessitates the reality of heaven. As for our part in heaven, the good news is that, if heaven is God's home, and God had human beings because He wanted to have children and share life and meaning with them, then it stands to reason that anyone who is truly a child of God can also rest with great assurance that they have a room reserved in heaven. Why? Because they are part of God's family and thus always welcome in God's home. Again, the grace part.

Now, given that, let's add one more complication, addressing the place of Hell. We have already established that the Christian God at least, as embodied in Christ, is necessarily characterized by love and grace, meaning God loves ALL of us simply because we exist. And, we have also discussed how God is not a manipulator of free will, as they would undermine the very reason He created us, to love. Jesus says God loves us as our Father, and Jesus' death on the cross makes it pretty clear how God feels about us.

By the way, if you want to know *how* Jesus is the Way, the Truth, and the Life, and no one gets to the Father except through Him, this is it. It is not some exclusionary statement that condemns all the world to a fate of hellfire and brimstone, even when many in that world love God more than life itself. No, Jesus is the *only Way* to God, because *grace* is the only way to God. In this, Jesus is the embodiment of grace, of unconditional love. Of course no one can get to the Father any other way, because without grace, there is not a person on the planet who is "good enough" to earn or merit God's love, and earn a place at God's table, in God's family.

You cannot earn "family." You are either born into it, or adopted into it, but you can never force, coerce, work your way into or manipulate yourself into someone else's family. No, they have to *want* you and accept you. Even more, show me any person in your own life that you truly love with all of your heart because they do things to impress you. Thank God he doesn't love us for our works, for we would all be doomed. No, God's love is far deeper and more profound than that. It is amazing grace. Which then, regarding our difficult questions about who gets into Heaven and Hell.

Who gets into Heaven? Who goes to Hell? Isn't this finally getting us to the point of God's inconsistency and why I should have legitimate concerns against Christianity? Well, maybe. But maybe not. I have already established that God already loves us all unconditionally. So that's the plumb line, and it will never change. Given that, it isn't like God is somehow going to "change His mind" about us (if so, it is not grace). So it stands to reason, the people who get into heaven (God's Home) are the very people who accept God's love and grace. They accept their place in God's family. And thus, they choose to be with God, with God's family, in God's home, forever.

But, this also is where the concept of Hell comes in. The idea being, God will never coerce, manipulate, or pull the puppet strings on people's free will to force them to accept His grace and their seat at His table or their room in God's heavenly home. God will not do that because, to do so, would undermine the very fabric of why God created us in the first place. You cannot love, truly love, without the true choice to hate. And you cannot love a robot or a puppet, for true love is relational. And you cannot force someone to love or be loving either. Seriously, try it. The next time you are in a fight with someone, lock them in a room until they come out "loving you." Just try forcing your own kid into "their room," when they did not choose to be there, and leave them there until they come out loving you and being grateful for your grace. Let me know, as Dr. Phil says, "how'd that work for you?" After forcing them to their "heavenly room," did they emerge with a great attitude of repentance and reconciliation and love, or did they come out angrier than a stirred up hornet's nest?

Free will. You cannot force anyone to feel anything, especially love. And the very second someone feels like you are trying to force or manipulate their feelings, they will defend themselves like a pinned down rattlesnake every time. Why this is true is because in the depths of our souls we are made to make choices with free will, and we feel it down to our bones. When people try to manipulate, suppress, oppress or coerce that free will, we buck, flinch, or just strike out every time. And yes, my hunch is, if God ever did that, we would wrestle with Him too. But although there are exceptions, usually God won't, because God wants us to love Him freely without feeling cornered and without coercion. And no matter how hard you try, because of free will, you cannot force someone else to love you. Love doesn't work that way.

Which leads to the final answer. We know what happens to people who love God and want to be in His family. Easy, they go to God's home, their home, with their family, in heaven. But, what happens to people who choose not to love God? What if they don't want to be in God's family? What if they want no part of living in God's presence for eternity? Is God supposed to lock them in their "heavenly room" until they come out wanting to be there, wanting to live in God's home, and even loving Him? Is that really what you would ask God to do, lock them in their room until they come out happy? No. And more, is that even fair to them and the free will God gave them, to try and force, coerce, and manipulate their free will, when they would not choose that option on their own in a million years? The answer is pretty apparent isn't it?   For people who choose to reject God's love, then they are also rejecting their place in God's family and, in turn, they are clearly saying they do not want to live with God in God's eternal home. Simply put, they don't want to be in God's home in heaven, and God won't force them to change their minds. What God does with people like that who reject Him? Honestly, let the theologians, denominations, and whoever work that out. Some Christians believe they go to "the place where God is not" (Hell), others believe they go to purgatory where they can repent and change, others believe in annihilation. We *do* know that God grieves for every lost sheep, that God as Father stands at the end of the street looking to the horizon hoping, longing, pleading for the prodigal to come home. Why? Because even if that man is out there rejecting His true family, rejecting His Father, rejecting His place at the table, and living in squalor, the Father still loves Him and wants Him back. Back where? Back home where he belongs. And for all eternity, that will never change.

Questions for Reflection (and discussion):

1. How does the existence of God relate to the existence of heaven?

2. What is heaven and why does heaven exist?

3. Who gets to go to heaven? Does everyone go to heaven? Why not?

4. How does human free will affect heaven?

5. Does God want anyone to *not* be in heaven? Why not?

Dr. Thomas Childs

NOTES

CHAPTER 6

What is God like?

Isaiah 9:6

"And He is called Wonderful Counselor, Mighty God, Everlasting Father, Prince of Peace."

Wwe've answered the question of God's existence, and we've addressed at least a few questions that relate to God and our world. But one of the most fundamental, important questions remains. What is God like?

Answer: *(Among other things)* ***Living Water, Bread of Life, Light of the World, Good Shepherd, Resurrection.***

I don't know if this has ever happened to you, but more and more these days, it seems that people like to put words in my mouth. It is almost a normal thing now, if you pause in the middle of a sentence to take a breath, someone else will almost always fill in the rest of the sentence for you. They assume they know what you are going to say. It is awkward at best when they assume you were going to say something you weren't. It is even worse when they assume you were going to say something that you believe is just plain wrong. What about you? Have you ever had anyone interrupt you mid-sentence and put words in your mouth?

Imagine with me for a moment. For whatever reason, daddy decides to let little Johnny walk up and down the cereal aisle in the grocery store to choose his own cereal. And as we all know, you have the plain, boxed bran and fiber cereals. You have the boring organic and multigrain cereals.

Then, you have the multicolored, 3D packaged, digitally mastered super chocolate, extra marshmallows rainbow colored Lucky Charms that are guaranteed to be magically delicious. And you even get a free leprechaun to boot. And of course, the kid yawns and fades on the organic and fiber cereals, but once you begin nearing the super chocolate Lucky Charms, it's like a dozing security guard rapid-fire chugging three *Monster* energy drinks. The sight line connects, and boom, "Dad, Dad, I want the super frosted chocolate-covered Lucky Charms! Yes, yes... that one." Thinking little of it, you buy it. After all, it's just a box of cereal, what's the worst that could happen? Right?

The first thing in the morning, little Johnny pops right out of bed and before the sleep is out of his eyes, he says, "Dad, Dad, can I have my super frosted, chocolate-covered marshmallow Lucky Charms?" Sure, Sure. Why not? And you fill the bowl with cereal and milk, and it's amazing. He never ate his other cereal like this. Wow, look at all the energy he is going to get from this full breakfast. And you pour another bowl until Johnny is finally satisfied, and all is well in the world. Off to school, and ready for a great day.

Then this. Let's assume little Johnny attends a fairly strict school, with very little tolerance for antics and misbehavior. Let's also imagine that Johnny gets certain "marks" when he misbehaves, and then his name on the board, and then a note in his folder to the parents. When daddy picks up from school little Johnny, who was filled up to his eyeballs on super chocolate frosted Lucky Charms that morning, what do you think was in his folder? A note from the teacher. As for how the day went? No happy face, instead marks on the board, name on the board, and this strange little note from the teacher that read, "Dear parents, please do not feed your children high sugar breakfasts before sending them to school. High sugar breakfasts make them hyper and irritable, etc." And no, hypothetically speaking, we don't think it's a good idea to feed little Johnny super frosted chocolate marshmallow Lucky Charms before school anymore.

Back to our story. The next morning, there are still some super frosted chocolate marshmallow Lucky Charms in the pantry. Little Johnny knows this. So what does he do? Once little Johnny sees that daddy is out of the room, he goes to mommy saying, "Mom, dad said I could have some chocolate Lucky Charms for breakfast. Is that OK?"

Long pause.

Then, with a roar that rivals Shrek when approached by a mob of villagers with pitchforks, "Daddy said what?!!!"

Ever had someone put words in your mouth? How did it make you feel when your words were twisted or completely made up? And do you notice, almost without exception, when someone puts words in your mouth, they have an agenda for themselves?

In my opinion, this is the real problem with people's perceptions of God today. Everyone knows about God. Everyone has heard something of God from this person or that person. Everyone has had a taste of something God-related, either through a religious experience (often boring), or a television show (even worse), some class in college taught by some off the wall professor, or just personal experiences that they found relevant. But when it comes to actually learning, paying attention to, and allowing space to hear from God, well, not so much.   In   this,   it   is becoming my increasing suspicion that far too many people have absolutely no clue what God says about Himself, and even worse, a part of them doesn't want to know. Why? They are afraid God isn't going to let them have their Lucky Charms. Even worse than that, deep down, we know the Lucky Charms aren't good for us, which compounds the issue further. And so what do we do? Unfortunately, we seek ways to ignore what is healthy, in hopes of getting whatever it is we   think   will   make   us   feel   good   in   the   moment. Theologically, this means we put words in God's mouth, making the True God into whatever it is we are wanting God to be, rather than what we really need.

Meet Jesus, as we know Him from the New Testament book of *John*. For our purposes, *John* gives us the best resource in the existence of the human race in understanding God. The reason is because, through *John*, God is talking to us about God's Self. In *John*, we are told that God was enfleshed in the person of Jesus Christ, that the Great "I Am" was literally walking and talking among us, and that God, in Christ, taught us about Himself. It is profound that *the* God, *the* Alpha and Omega, *the* Creator of it all, walked around in the flesh, spent time with us, and taught us about Himself. And that's our focus here. With the book of *John*, no longer are we dealing with assumptions, speculation, and sincere, but misguided interpretations of God. No, *John* gives us God from God's own mouth.

Let me put this another way. John is a theology book. *Theos* meaning "God," and *logos* meaning "study of or truth about." So when theologians call John a theology book, they in essence are saying that John is a study of God, His nature, attributes, so on and so forth. But the interesting piece is that, where some would expect a theology book to be discussing some esoteric, mythical God, the book of *John* in fact is discussing a real life, in the flesh, eating, drinking, and breathing human being--Jesus. And as CS Lewis says in his *Mere Christianity* masterpiece, this is precisely what Jesus intended for us to understand. Jesus left us no other options for who He claimed to be. Jesus left no other option, than these: He is God, or He is a fraud or liar. Call Him a fake? Ok. Call Him a liar? That's definitely an option. Call Jesus a demon-spawn from Hell? Your call. But don't ever call Him just great teacher or some "cool dude" or spiritual guru. Why? Well, because of what Jesus Himself said.

So what did Jesus say? And why should we care? We start with what he said. And just think this one through for yourself. Why was Jesus crucified? You really don't even need to look anywhere else for this one. Did Jesus murder anyone? Did He steal, or lie, or cheat, or rob a bank, or sell drugs, or anything else like that? Answer: Of course not. In his very real life, He was a model citizen. Well, almost. Yes,

Jesus was an amazingly gracious and loving man, model citizen, and even fantastic ethicist and moralist. But here's the thing, He also claimed to be God.

Jesus claimed to be God. This is why He was crucified. There is no denying it and there is no middle ground. He said that He was the very same Being as Whoever it was that told Moses from the burning bush that "I Am that I Am." Jesus literally said, "before Abraham was, I Am." Jesus also said, "I and the Father are one and the same." Seriously? If I were to preface this book by telling you that the Great "I Am" and I are one and the same, how would you feel about that? For most people, you'd say, put him in the nuthouse. Which, by the way, is what some people thought about Jesus. Regarding many others, he just made terrible enemies. And they crucified Him for it. But for others, they loved Him for it, because the words He spoke rang true. And, because He met their needs and answered their questions only as God could.

Living Water. John 4:10,26. Try to walk in the shoes of the pariah, Samaritan woman that Jesus met at the well. She had been married and divorced several times, maybe a husband or two had died on her, and she was living with someone who was not her husband in a society that ostracized and shunned such women. For her, Jesus filled her soul, made her feel valued and loved by God, and, according to Jesus, He became her Living Water. Living Water. Interesting, because Jesus is saying, I am like Living Water, which means God is like Living Water, filling that deep thirst within all of us, if we are willing to receive what He is offering.

Bread of Life. John 6:35. Jesus fed 5,000 people from a few loaves of bread and a few fish. Later, they would come back to Jesus, wanting more bread, because they were still hungry. Jesus said that they, in truth, had a deep hunger that no earthly bread could fill. "I Am Bread of Life," Jesus would tell them. Meaning, God is Bread of Life, satisfying that deep hunger and lack of true satisfaction within all human beings, if we are willing to receive what He is offering.

Light of the World. John 8:12. Can you imagine being caught in the act of adultery by your enemies, much less your spouse? And not only that, but then your enemies grab you by the hair, drag you (probably naked) into a public street. You are screaming, and weeping, and getting bruised and battered by the cobblestones. You think they may even kill you, until you realize, of all places, they are taking you to the holiest religious site in the city. A place filled with hundreds of people. Horribly humiliating. And they throw you at the feet of this man, Jesus, who is teaching a large crowd in the Temple. It truly must have been the darkest day of that poor woman's life.

Accusations are lodged. And this Jesus, in the midst of your devastating chaos, Jesus bends down, draws in the dirt, and miraculously gets all those accusers to shut up, completely walk away and leave you alone.

And there you are. Lying prostrate on the ground. Weeping, sobbing, humiliated, shamed, bruised, and battered. You continue sobbing for a while. Maybe someone brings you a blanket or whatever to cover yourself in the meantime. Who knows. Either way, Jesus patiently waits. And after a time, as you begin to find your dignity, Jesus asks you a question, "Woman, where are your accusers?" "They have left," you say. Jesus responds, "Yes, yes they have." A few more tears fall. "I want you to know something," Jesus continues. "Yes?" from the woman. Perhaps she is staring at the dirt, perhaps she is in such shock that the words are a muddled hum of chaotic noise. So to get her attention, can you see it? Jesus walk up to the woman, He crouches to his knees, he lifts her chin so she will see His eyes, and with a grace and compassion that surpasses what any words on a page could ever describe, Jesus says, "It's OK. It really is going to be OK." And here is what she feels, *light* and warmth.

And yes, I know the "Go home and sin no more part." Fine. But notice where all this is headed. Personally, I think that woman was still sitting there at the feet of Jesus when He said the next part. Because I think He meant it for her when He said, "I Am the *Light* of the World." I Am, God Is, Light. And not just any light, but *The* Light. The Light that takes the darkest day or the darkest night, the Light that takes the most horrific darkness, and in that darkness, *Light* shines.

Jesus was saying, "Woman... you who have been battered, bruised and on this very day living a darkness of personal Hell that few understand... to you I AM Light of the World." If only you will let me. And she did. And my hunch is, her life was forever transformed. Interesting. Interesting, because Jesus is saying, I am like that. God is like that. Light of the World, which means God is Light of the World, bringing light and warmth to our cold and dark days, if we are willing to receive what He is offering.

Good Shepherd. John 10:11. A man had lived his entire life never being able to see. And then he runs into Jesus (God), and he is both healed and given spiritual sight. Jesus says, I Am, God Is like that, like a Good Shepherd who leads notoriously blind sheep (humans) to the place where they can truly see.

Resurrection. John 11:25. Mary and Martha experienced God when their brother and provider Lazarus was raised from the dead. Now that's an interesting role-play. Imagine being a woman who was taken care of, provided for, your entire life by your oldest brother. The society you live in has made it clear, without a man by your side, you are worthless. All you have is Lazarus. And then he dies. Imagine the grief, the pain, and the worry about how you will live. What next? But then Jesus (God) comes along, and He literally raises Lazarus back to life from the dead. And all your worries, about death and ultimate loss, gone. I Am like that, Jesus says, for "I Am the Resurrection and the Life."

And all those things got Jesus what? Crucified. Which tells us even more of what God is like. Because before he was crucified, Jesus said, "Greater love no one has, than to lay your life down for your friends." And then from the cross where He was crucified *as* he was being crucified, Jesus would say, "Father forgive them, for they know not what they do." Truly, truly amazing.

And don't get hung up on Jesus talking to the Father, which makes them different. Of course they were different, but that doesn't mean they still didn't have the exact same substance and essence. They did, and that is how Jesus was God. Different in form, but exactly the same in substance and essence. And that makes all the difference in the world.

Why? Because when it was all said and done, this tells us that God loves us unconditionally. That, even when we are at our worst, even when we are the consummate prodigal and crucifying God Himself, God still looks at us with longing and grace. If only, if only we would accept the truth of who we are, behave like it, and come home. Which really brings us to the ultimate question of this book.

Christian Logic. As it has been, so it is, so it always will be. Two plus two equals four, and when you combine the exact same ingredients under the exact same conditions, you will always get the exact same results. These truths about God have not and will not change. This is the part of God's nature that is incredibly assuring and comforting to us humans who tend to be so unstable. Of course, we *like to think* we are stable, and especially in our seasons of stability, we tend to do all in our power to find all we want and need without God's help. And in so doing, we will often cast Him aside and act as if His life and existence doesn't matter. We often will convince ourselves that God's logic and truth are not relevant. But the reality is, it *is* relevant, and it *does* matter.

Anyone who has lived long enough to experience that "hole in your heart" knows exactly what I am saying. It is a hole that no career, house, car, bank account, job, spouse, kids, or whatever else can fill. It is a hole of discontentment, uneasiness, and angst that nothing in the world can fill. Which is precisely what God intends, because He wants us to turn to Him to fill it. It is a hole that only God's love, the love of our true Father, can fill. It is Living Water and so much more. It is what we are searching for (His love). He is *Our Father,* and He created us to need Him and His love, precisely because He loves us so much. This means, we need Water, Bread, Light, Sight, and Resurrection. Can you enjoy a season or two without it? Sure. But long term, without connecting to the Source, the Vine from which all those blessings flow, your life will forever be missing something, the engine will conk.

What if God actually wants something better for you? Christian Logic says God is offering you a better life, even if it might not look like what you expect. It is *not* that the answers do not exist. They do. It is *not* that God is doing everything in His power to help you see the logic of those answers, for He is. But you have free will, and we have already discussed the implications of what that means. Ultimately, it means you must choose to accept the answers that God provides. It is faith, seeking understanding. And when we combine the two, there is no question that your life will be transformed.

So, ask your questions. Seek understanding. Never stop using your brain, even put a little faith *in* that brain you have. Just remember who it is who gave you that brain in the first place, and have faith in Him too. And when the combination of faith and logic leads you to answers that finally make sense of the ultimate questions you have in life, accept those answers. For in accepting those answers, you in fact, are accepting not just Christian Logic, but the unconditional love of the very God who calls you his child, and who has been longing for a meaningful relationship with you since before the day you were born.

Questions for Reflection (and discussion):

1. How do you currently think of God? How would you describe God to someone else?

2. How do the descriptors from Jesus, in John, affect your thinking about God?

      a. Living Water?

      b. Bread of Life?

      c. Light of the World?

      d. Good Shepherd?

      e. Resurrection?

3. If God really was enfleshed in Christ, and He had the power to change it, what does the crucifixion of Christ say about the depth of God's love for you and your loved ones?

4. How might God's love make a real difference for your own life today?

NOTES

Available on
Audible & Ebook!

Look for:

CHRISTIAN LOGIC 2
CHRISTIAN LOGIC 3

FB: Dr. Thomas Childs

ABOUT THE AUTHOR

Dr. Thomas Childs grew up in Fairhope, Alabama, attending Baldwin county schools before graduating from Fairhope High School. He earned a B.M. degree in Jazz Studies (magna cum laude) from Loyola University, New Orleans, a Master of Divinity Degree (with biblical languages) from Southwestern Baptist Theological Seminary in Fort Worth, TX, studied at the Goethe Institute in Manheim Germany for a Summer, a Master of Theological Studies (cum laude) from Perkins School of Theology at Southern Methodist University, and his Doctorate of Ministry Degree (with honors) from St Paul School of Theology in Missouri.

Thomas has toured with the Christian band TRUTH, as well as playing in the New Orleans Symphony, the New Orleans Saints Jazz Band, the Desire Brothers band, the Harmon Lights jazz band, and others. Additionally, Thomas was the first chair trumpet player in the state of Alabama All-State competition, first chair in the Southern United States Honor Band, and the Outstanding Music Major for Loyola Univ in 1993.

Thomas' church resume includes being the founding pastor of the LifePoint United Methodist Church, as well as being the pastor of the Dido United Methodist Church, the Blooming Grove United Methodist Church, and the Dresden United Methodist Church.

Thomas received the 2000 Morris Walker Clergy award for the Central Texas Conference of the United Methodist Church. Thomas has been an adjunct faculty for teaching

Christian Leadership in the clinical pastoral education program at Harris Methodist Hospital, as well as teaching Christian Leadership at Texas Wesleyan University.

Thomas also has served as the Director of the St Andrews UMC building project in the Waxahachie District of the Central TX Conference in 1998-1999, as well as serving as the Host Operations Director for the 2008 General Conference of the United Methodist Church in Fort Worth, TX from 2004-2008.

Thomas is married to Dr. Gladys Childs and together they have one son, Scott Childs.

Made in the USA
Columbia, SC
07 April 2018